Creepy Creatures

Cockroaches

Nancy Dickmann

Raintree

Chicago, Illinois

Printed and bound by South China Printing Company.
10 09 08 07 06
10 9 8 7 6 5 4 3 2 1

Library of Congress Cataloging-in-Publication Data:
Dickmann, Nancy.
  Cockroaches / Nancy Dickmann.
    p. cm. -- (Creepy creatures)
  Includes index.
  ISBN 1-4109-1769-X (library binding - hardcover) -- ISBN 1-4109-1774-6 (pbk.)
  1. Cockroaches--Juvenile literature. I. Title. II. Series.

QL505.5.D53 2006
595.7'28--dc22

                                          2005012452

Acknowledgments
The publishers would like to thank the following for permission to reproduce photographs: Alamy Images pp. 19 (Daniel L Geiger/SNAP), 21 (James Caldwell); Corbis pp. 15, 22 (FLPA); Getty Images pp. 4, 5, 23; Natural Visions p. 20 (Heather Angel); Nature Picture Library p. 9; Oxford Scientific Films pp. 7 (Animals Animals), 8 (Animals Animals), 10–11 (Animals Animals), 14 (Paulo de Oliveira), 16–17 (Waina Cheng), 18, 23 (Brian Kenney); Photolibrary p. 6; Science Photolibrary p. 13 (Martin Dohrn); Woodfall Wildlife Images p. 12 (John Robinson).

Cover picture of a cockroach reproduced with permission of Dwight Kuhn.

Every effort has been made to contact copyright holders of any material reproduced in this book.
Any omissions will be rectified in subsequent printings if notice is given to the publishers.

Some words are shown in *bold*, **like this**. You can find out what they mean by looking in the glossary on page 24.

Contents

Cockroaches

Cockroaches are a kind of insect.

Have you ever seen a cockroach?

Looking for Cockroaches

Cockroaches like to live where it is warm and dark.

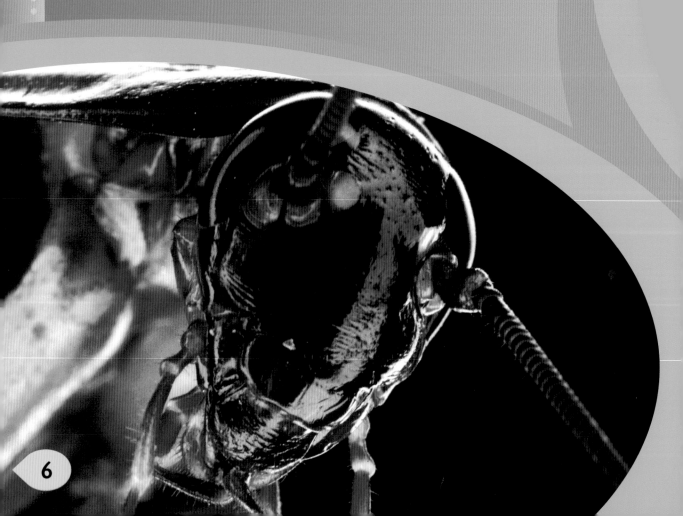

They often hide in our homes.

Cockroaches in the Wild

Some cockroaches live in the **rain forest**.

They are brightly colored.

9

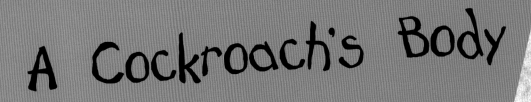

A Cockroach's Body

Cockroaches have *flat* bodies.

Can you count the legs?

They have two **antennae** for smelling.

Cockroaches on the Move

Cockroaches can run *fast*.

Most cockroaches can also fly.

Cockroach Eggs

The female cockroach carries her eggs in **pouches**.

soft white babies **hatch** from the eggs.

Young Cockroaches

Soon the baby cockroaches turn brown.

They grow and grow and grow.

16

They **shed** their skin when it gets too small.

Food for Cockroaches

Cockroaches will eat almost anything.

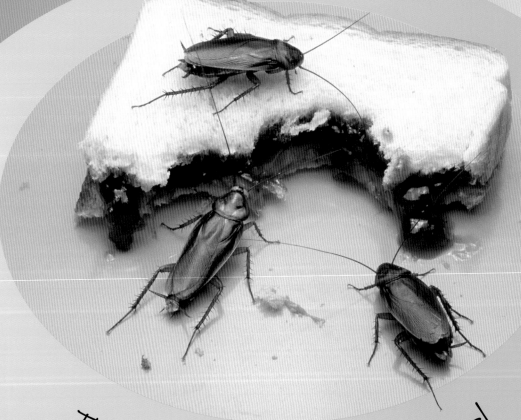

They even eat jelly sandwiches!

Cockroaches usually eat at night.

Cockroaches in Danger

Spiders and other animals eat cockroaches.

Cockroaches look for small cracks to hide in.

Types of Cockroaches

There are thousands of kinds of cockroaches.

They live all over
the world.

Glossary

antenna (More than one are antennae.) feeler on an insect's head that helps it smell, see, or hear

hatch to come out of an egg

pouch place for carrying something

rain forest thick, jungly forest where lots of rain falls

shed to lose an old layer of skin when a new, bigger one has grown

Index

Notes for Adults

This series supports the young child's exploration of their learning environment and their knowledge and understanding of their world. Using the books in the series together will enable comparison of similarities and differences to be made. (NB. Many of the photographs in **Creepy Creatures** show them much larger than life size. The first spread of each title shows the creature at approximately its real life size.)

This book introduces the reader to the life cycle and behavior of the cockroach. It will also help children extend their vocabulary as they hear new words like *rain forest*, *antennae*, and *hatch*. You may like to introduce and explain other new words yourself, like *habitat*, *larva*, and *molt*.

Additional Information

Cockroaches are medium-sized insects; some live near people and others are tropical. All cockroaches prefer a warm, dark, humid environment. The male usually has two pairs of wings; females are either wingless or have vestigial wings. The tropical species are often brightly colored. All cockroaches are fast runners and many types can fly, some for long distances. A female carries eggs in egg cases that protrude from her body. After she deposits an egg case, soft white nymphs appear. They go through several molts before becoming adults. Every time a cockroach molts the new cuticle is white but turns brown within a few hours. Cockroaches are scavengers; they eat human food and many other things including paper, soap, plants, and dead animals. They are most active at night.

Follow-up Activities

Can the children think of other animals or insects with many legs?

• Can the children think of other animals or insects that might live in a house?

• Draw, paint, or make models of cockroaches.

• Read a fictional story such as *Leo Cockroach: Toy Tester* by Kevin O'Malley, and ask the children to relate the events to factual information in this book.